UNDER THE MYRTLE TREE

A COMPILATION OF HEART-WARMING LOVE POEMS.

SHARVEE

to every soul, inspiring the poet in me

and

to all my fellow romantics.

Contents

Contents

Acknowledgements

First and foremost I would like to thank my family for supporting me through this journey and providing me with the necessary resources to publish my book . I am most grateful to all the beautiful people who inspired the romantic in me to write these poems. A huge thank you to my English teacher for assisting and reviewing this book. I am also thankful to the poet, Atticus, whose book "The dark between stars" sparked the desire in me to write this book.

Prologue

What is love?

What does love feel like?

How do you know you're in love?

Imagine a girl sitting under a Myrtle tree. Shes furiously scribbling something in a black notebook. She lives through her poetry, the romance she has created inside her head seems almost impossible for anybody to fullfill...or maybe not? Maybe the meaning of love for her will change as she grows up or maybe she'll have the same innocent way of looking at it. What does she think about love though? What is love to her?

Chapter 1

You outdid the clouds,
That were pretty as ever.
Your angelic smile,
Your twinkling eyes,
I wish u could see,
the beauty in you,
I wish u could believe,
my words were true.

Chapter2

He felt like a warm shower,
Sinking into his arms,
His eyes like my morning coffee,
Gazing into the black softness.
His soul pure like the bright blue sky,
Laying my head on his firm chest,
Darling oh my lover,
I wish to be with you forever.

Chapter3

How do I tell you that it's okay to try,
To melt into me,hold you close when you cry.
It's okay to show me who you really are,
I promise to love you and kiss all your scars.

Chapter4

I woke up wanting you,
I went to sleep wanting you,
My heart my mind my soul,
Craving your love and you.
Oh but maybe the truth is,
I always wanted you.

Chapter5

You are like a beautiful painting,
You my darling are a work of art.
So perfectly and carefully sculpted,
You deserve the biggest canvas.

Chapter 6

If I gave you my heart,
Would you keep it safe,
Would you look after it,
And make sure it doesn't break.
Would you treasure it forever and ever and ever,
Would you love me forever and ever and ever.

Chapter7

Fall into my arms my love,
That so want to hold you close.
Look into my eyes my love,
That so want to get lost in your gaze.
My arms will never let you go,
My eyes will never look at anyone else.
Trust me my love,
I promise you'll never be hurt again.

Chapter8

Running my hands through your hair,
As you lay asleep in my lap.
Admiring your beautiful face,
Kissing your forehead, I whispered...
"I want to spend the rest of our life
Deeply in love with each other...
I want to spend the rest of our life
Together..
..forever."

Chapter 9

Words I want to say to you,
Are words written in my poems.
Things I want to do with you,
Are things done in my poems.
Can you tell they're about you?
Can you tell I've fallen for you.

Chapter10

I admire you from afar,
Though my heart aches to be near.
I long to be close enough,
To caress your face,
And tell you...
How much I really adore you.

Chapter 11

You brought back the child in me,
She giggled and danced and sang around you,
Her heart pure and bursting with love,
She didn't hold back around you.
My little girl you set her free.
My little girl she finally felt peace.

Chapter12

Our hands locked as we dance in the living room.

Our eyes locked as you pull me close, hand on my waist.

Our hearts locked as I rest my head ,

On your chest.

I wish I could stay in this moment,

Till the end of time with you.

Chapter13

Too many things to say about you,
Too many ways you make me feel.
I see you smile and I think to myself,
How grateful I am to have you with me,
How grateful I am to spend my life with you.

Chapter14

We could write our very own fairytale,
A happy beginning,
And a happy ending.
Sail through trouble,
Like a ship riding the storm.
Run away from the world,
Escape to a far away land.
Be each other's home,
Be each other's hope,
Be each other's reason,
To believe in love.

Chapter15

Four words is all it will take,
For me to be with you forever.
I belong to you then,
I would be yours to keep then.
So say the four words and take my heart,
"Will you be mine?" And then I'm all yours.

Chapter16

Run into my arms you said,
Squeeze you tight and never let go,
Stay there in the safety of your embrace,
And let our hearts connect.

Chapter 17

Our hands touch and sparks r felt,
Our eyes meet and a connection is formed.
Our hearts joined a new love is born,
Our souls are tangled, our future is formed.

Chapter18

Your voice like wine,
Cooled for a long time.
I wish to get drunk and lose myself,
The thirst will never be quenched.
I wish to get drunk and give myself,
To you to keep for the rest of our life.

Chapter19

The love we share runs so deep,
Deeper than the greed,
For materialistic things.
The love we share runs so deep,
We could have nothing,
Yet...
Have everything we need.

Chapter20

I could buy every flower in the world for you,
I could sing every love song to you,
I could write a million poems for you,
But it wouldn't be enough to tell,
How much I really love you.

Chapter21

I love you with all of my heart,
Till the day my heart stops beating.
I love you with my mind,
Till the day my mind might forget.
I love you with my soul,
And will always love you then.

Chapter 22

Our love is simple,
Our love is pure,
Our love is loyal,
Our love is real.
There will be pain,
There will be heartbreak,
There will be times,
Where we scream and cry.
But there will never be separation,
Never a doubt,
Our love is strong.
Our love is forever.

Chapter23

You made my lonely nights,
Full of joy and comfort.
You made my rainy days,
Full of sunshine and peace.
You made my broken heart,
Hopeful of being fixed again.

Chapter24

The way birds welcome the first rays of the sun,
The way crops welcome the first shower of rain,
The way summer is welcomed after a cold winter,
The same way my heart always welcomes you.

Chapter 25

Your eyes twinkled like the stars in the sky,
Your voice gentle like the whispering Wind.
I could stay here all night long,
In the warmth of your soft embrace.

Chapter26

You smell like the fresh earth after a shower of rain,
Like the sweet smell of flowers and leaves,
Like the smell of a freshly baked cake,
So soft and sweet and pure,
I wish to preserve your smell,
And keep it with me always.

Chapter27

The sun set slowly through the rocks,
As you kissed me, so gentle and promising.
The flame ignited eternal and strong,
A fiery passion burned between us.

Chapter28

And when he looked at me,
His face so close to mine...
I felt myself blush,
With a different type of warmth...
Oh, to caress his face,
Like admiring the beauty of a flower.

Chapter29

He said i had the most wonderful smile,
But little did he know....
He was the only reason i smiled and laughed,
He was my happy place after all.

Chapter30

Let your thorns prick me,
For after the pain comes the beauty,
The beauty of the rose,
The beauty of your love.

Chapter 31

Trust....
Trust in me, trust in my love.
Trust in my words, trust in my touch.
Because your happiness is mine,
And I'd like to think, your heart is mine too.

Chapter32

Through my hearts window,
A dove sings its songs of love,
Opening the window to your heart,
You sing along to the notes,
Of our loves harmony, eternal.

Thankyou